P9-DNS-667

Will You Marry Me?

Will You Marry Me?

SEVEN CENTURIES OF LOVE

WILLIAMSBURG REGIONAL LIBRARY
7770 CROAKER ROAD
WILLIAMSBURG, VIRGINIA 23188

APR 2008

Edited by

HELENE SCHEU-RIESZ

A TOUCHSTONE BOOK
PUBLISHED BY SIMON & SCHUSTER
New York London Toronto Sydney

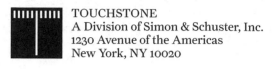 TOUCHSTONE
A Division of Simon & Schuster, Inc.
1230 Avenue of the Americas
New York, NY 10020

Copyright 1940 by Helene Scheu-Riesz

All rights reserved, including the right to reproduce this book or
portions thereof in any form whatsoever. For information address
Touchstone Subsidiary Rights Department,
1230 Avenue of the Americas, New York, NY 10020.

First Touchstone hardcover edition January 2008

TOUCHSTONE and colophon are registered
trademarks of Simon & Schuster, Inc.

For information about special discounts for bulk purchases,
please contact Simon & Schuster Special Sales at 1-800-456-6798
or business@simonandschuster.com.

Designed by Jill Weber

Manufactured in the United States of America

1   3   5   7   9   10   8   6   4   2

The Library of Congress has cataloged the
Island Press edition as follows:
Scheu-Riesz, Helene, ed.
Will you marry me?
p. cm.
1. Love-letters. 2. Courtship. I. Title.
PN6140.L7 S35 1944
808.86 44-7657

ISBN-13: 978-1-4165-4009-0
ISBN-10: 1-4165-4009-1

Contents

Will You Marry Me?

Introduction

ARRIAGE IS BECOMING FASHIONABLE again, after an age of barnstorming revolutionists who looked for other ways of keeping the race going. It is taught at universities as a science; it is practiced in life and literature as an art. That is one of the reasons why a collection of proposal letters seems timely.

Many volumes of love letters have been published in English, but so far as I could discover, no proposal letters. The reasons are evident. Such letters are rare; people who write or receive them are seldom willing to exhibit them. Yet the few available are much more illuminating of personalities than any other documents they left. They show men and women at the crossroads of their lives, before the ultimate decision that will shape their own future and that of humanity insofar as they are part of it.

Love letters are as uniform as the passion that creates them. Proposals reflect social background; they picture society.

It has often been said that life copies art. Schools of painting have changed the faces and figures of men and women. Novels have created types of lovers. Churches, palaces, and homes have influenced the development of people who lived around and in them. This shows in proposal letters; their style follows the style of architecture. The square heavy construction of the early Norman cathedral; the mystic upward swing of the slender Gothic arch; the clear classical stability of the Renaissance pillar; the round arches, turrets, vaults, bulging ornaments, and trumpeting angels of the Baroque; the fantastic grace and freakishness of the Rococo; the Puritan simplicity, religious devotion, and economic shrewdness of the early American colonists; and the eclecticism, imitation, and promiscuousness in styles of later colonists—all can be traced in the proposal letters through the centuries. Cathedrals, fortresses, palaces, mansions, parliaments, log cabins, cottages, and apartment houses rise behind them and form the background to the individual fate of famous men and women who asked the big question.

The pendulum of emotional expression swings between overstatement and understatement, romanticism and realism. Victorian prudery was followed by Edwardian license, and this again gives way to the spirit that prompts a king to give up his throne rather than be united to the woman he loves by a ceremony less binding than a church wedding.

Experts say that the history of evolution nearly always shows the male as the leader in the marriage game because he likes to hunt while the female prefers to be hunted. But if Hollywood pictures are a true reflection of contemporary life, the game has been reversed. The majority show the hero as the hunted party. The heroine often needs a full evening's program to break his resistance. Is this the reality of a functional age or only dream and wish fulfillment?

The polar explorer Sir Hubert Wilkins once told me how penguins propose.

When a male penguin meets a female attractive enough to make him think of marriage, he picks up a pebble from the ground and places it at her feet. She looks him over, and if she thinks he will do, she accepts the token and carries it to a secluded spot among the rocks where she would like to reside; there and then the nest is built and family life started.

A Scott-Peary expedition to the South Pole had a painter along who used to sit sketching among the rocks. One morning a penguin came along and put a pebble down at his feet.

Sir Hubert did not say whether the painter accepted the token or just made a sketch of the wayward suitor.

According to the animal biographer Brehm, birds are the leaders in monogamy. They live in the only true marriage; they mate for life. Their proposals are recorded in music, and it is still the male who sings them.

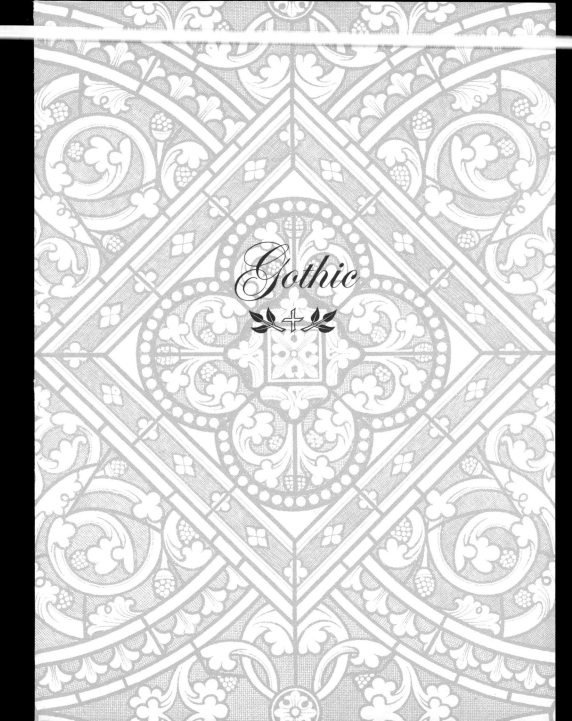

*L*ETTER WRITING DID NOT BECOME a general practice before the discovery of America. Not that the art of writing is new! The tombs of Egypt yield bronze pens of the best workmanship, but the Pharaohs have left no private correspondence. The parchments found in the pyramids are bills and accounts of household matters.

The earliest letter of proposal that can be traced was probably the epistle King David sent to his general Joab, when Bathsheba, the wife of Uriah, had taken the royal fancy.

 It is a grim proposal by proxy.

David to Joab, sent by the hand of Uriah the Hittite

1035 BC

*S*et ye Uriah in the forefront of the hottest battle, and retire ye from him that he may be smitten, and die.

Seeing that such use was made of the technique of writing, it is not astonishing that the Greeks, when it was introduced into their country about that time, looked upon it as something evil—the way alchemy and astrology were looked upon later in history. Many of the early letters pertaining to royal marriages bear out the sinister meaning of the word "runic." Archives of the courts still reveal cartloads of information illuminating the dark ages when kingdoms could only be acquired by war or marriage—equally cruel—and when it was customary to get rid of enemies, wives, or husbands by poison.

One of these letters, though not a proposal in the strict sense, throws so much light upon the way marriages were proposed and settled at the time that it seems to belong here to paint the background.

Isabella of Angoulême, as a young child, had been engaged to Hugh de Lusignan, a Norman nobleman, and given into his custody. When she was twelve, King John of England demanded her hand in marriage, and her father, preferring a king as a son-in-law, took her away from Lusignan. To appease his fury, the first daughter of John and Isabella was, from the cradle, engaged to him.

King John was not easy to live with. Far from faithful him-self, he was jealous and had a habit of hanging his wife's ad-mirers at the head of her bed. When he died—poisoned by a monk for trying to rape the abbot's sister—Isabella quickly robbed her infant daughter of her fiancé and married him herself. Her letter to her young son Henry III neatly explains how she did it all in pure, unselfish, motherly devotion.

Isabella of Angoulême, Queen Dowager and
Countess of March and Angoulême,
to King Henry of England

AD 1220

*W*e hereby signify to you that when the Earls of
March and Eu departed this life, the Lord Hugh de
Lusignan remained alone and without heirs in Poictou, and his friends would not permit that our daughter should be united to him by marriage, because her
age is so tender, but counseled him to take a wife from
whom he might speedily hope for an heir; and it was
proposed that he should take a wife in France, which
if he had done, all your land in Poictou and Gascony
should be lost. We therefore, seeing the great peril that
might accrue to you if that marriage took place, married the said Hugh Earl of March ourselves; and God
knows that we rather did it for your benefit than our
own. Wherefore we entreat you, as our dear son, that
this thing may be pleasing to you, seeing that it con-
duces greatly to the profit of you and yours; and we
earnestly pray that you restore to him his lawful right,
that is Niort, the castles of Exeter and Rockingham,
and 3,500 marks which your father, our former hus-

band, bequeathed to us; and so, if it please you, deal with him who is so powerful, that he may not remain against you, since he can serve you well . . . and if it shall please you, you may send for our daughter, your sister, by a trusty messenger and letters patent, and we will send her to you.

Isabella was beautiful and mischievous. She did not send her daughter but kept her as a sort of hostage, to put pressure on the king, her son. She intrigued against him and put all sorts of difficulties in his way.

The plight in which Margery Brews, who later became Mrs. John Paston, found herself when she wrote the following letter is an example of what marriages mostly were concerned with in the fifteenth century, among wealthy commoners as among royalty.

Unto my right well-beloved Valentine, John Paston Esqu., be this bill delivered:

1477

*R*ight reverend and worshipful and right-beloved Valentine, I recommend me to you full heartily, desiring to hear of your welfare, which I beseech the Almighty God long for to preserve.... And if it please you to hear of my welfare, I am not in good health of body nor heart nor shall be till I hear from you.

And my lady my mother hath belabored the matter to my father full diligently, but she can no more get than ye know of; for which God knoweth I am full sorry. But if ye love me as I trust verily that ye do, ye will not leave me therefore. For if ye had not half the livelihood that ye have for to do the greatest labor that any woman alive might, I would not forsake you.

No more to you at this time, but the Holy Trinity have you in keeping. And I beseech you that this bill be not seen by none earthly creature save yourself.

And this letter was indited at Topcroft, with full heavy heart

BY YOUR OWN
Margery Brews

Arthur, Prince of Wales, eldest son of Henry VII, was engaged to the Spanish princess Catherine of Aragon. Her parents, Ferdinand and Isabella, postponed the marriage for two years, till the bridegroom had completed his fourteenth year and the bride was fifteen.

They were married in November 1501, and five months later Catherine was a widow. Henry VII was so afraid that he would have to pay back Catherine's dowry and would lose the alliance with Spain that he urged the engagement of his second son, Henry, to the young widow. That the boy was only eleven at the time and Catherine seventeen did not hinder the father and Catherine's friends both in England and in Spain from campaigning for a speedy celebration of the marriage. Special permission had to be obtained from the pope, who was glad to give it because he hoped the union would strengthen the Roman Church in England. Young Henry resisted for a while and registered doubts about the validity of such a marriage, but he married Catherine in the end.

Arthur, Prince of Wales, to Catherine of Aragon

1499

*M*ost illustrious and excellent lady, my dearest spouse,

I wish you very much health. . . . I have read the sweet letters of your Highness, from which I have easily perceived your entire love for me. Truly your letters traced by your own hand have so delighted me and have rendered me so cheerful and jocund that I fancied I beheld your Highness and conversed with and beheld my dearest wife. I cannot tell you what an earnest desire I feel to see your Highness, and how vexatious is to me this procrastination of your coming . . . let it be hastened that instead of absent we may be present with each other, and the loves conceived between us may reap their proper fruit. . . .

From our castle of Ludlow,
5th of October 1499

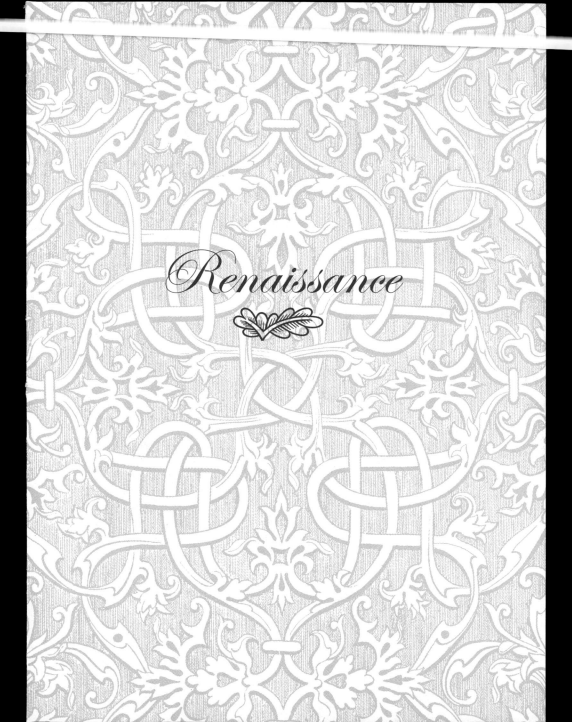

Renaissance

Henry VIII was the first English king raised in the ideas of the Renaissance. Had Catherine given him the son he craved, the schism which brought about the founding of the Church of England might never have occurred. As it was, Henry broke away from Catherine and the pope at the same time. The next letter shows how he wooed Anne Boleyn, the second lady on his long marriage list.

Henry married Anne in 1533 and had her beheaded in 1536. Only a few months after having made her his queen, he was writing letters of the same kind to her successor, Jane Seymour.

 Henry VIII to Anne Boleyn

   UNDATED, BEFORE 1533

*B*y revolving in my mind the contents of your last letters, I have put myself into great agony, not knowing how to interpret them, whether to my disadvantage (as I understood some others) or not. I beseech you earnestly to let me know your real mind as to the love between us two. It is needful for me to obtain this answer from you, having been for a whole year wounded with the dart of love and not yet assured whether I shall succeed in finding a place in your heart and affections. This uncertainty has hindered me of late from declaring you my mistress . . . lest it should prove that you only entertain an ordinary regard for me. But if you please to do the duty of a true and loyal mistress and to give yourself heart and person to me, who will be, as I have been, your most loyal servant (if your rigor does not forbid me), I promise you that not only the name shall be given you but also that I will take you for my mistress, cutting off all others that are in competition with you, out of my thoughts and affections, and serving you only. I beg you to give an entire answer to this my rude letter, that I may know on what and how far I may depend; but if it does not please you to answer me in writing, let me know some place where I may have it by word of mouth, and I will go thither with all my heart.

No more for fear of tiring you. Written by the hand of him who will willingly remain

YOUR
Henry Rex

As described by a contemporary, Jane Seymour was not strik-ing. Of middle height and pallid complexion, she was not con-sidered beautiful. "She is twenty-five," Chapuys says of her, "and you may imagine whether she, being an Englishwoman and having been so long at court, would not hold it a sin to be still a maid. At which the king will be rather pleased . . . for he will marry her on condition she is a virgin, and when he wants a divorce, he will find plenty of witnesses to the contrary."

But Jane, contrary to these expectations, escaped the fates of Catherine and Anne. More than any of his other wives, Henry loved Jane and mourned her when she died in child-birth—giving him the son he craved.

 Henry VIII to Jane Seymour

   1536

My dear friend and mistress,

The bearer of these few lines from thy entirely devoted servant will deliver into thy fair hands a token of my true affection for thee, hoping you will keep it forever in your sincere love for me. Advertising you that there is a ballad made lately of great derision against us, which if it go much abroad and is seen by you, I pray you to pay no manner of regard to it. I am not at present informed who is the setter forth of this malignant writing, but if he is found out, he shall be straitly punished for it. For the things ye lacked, I have minded my lord to supply them to you as soon as he can buy them. Thus hoping shortly to receive you in these arms, I am for the present

YOUR OWN LOVING SERVANT AND SOVEREIGN

Henry Rex

Realism had won the fight against mysticism when Anne Boleyn's daughter, Elizabeth, ascended the throne. Young, charming, queen of a rich and powerful realm, she was the most attractive prize on the marriage market where alliances decided the fate of nations. But she was averse to marriage, or appeared to be so.

Immediately after the death of her father, Elizabeth received a proposal from the admiral of the fleet, one of Jane Seymour's brothers. She refused him and he consoled himself with her father's widow, Catherine Parr. This early experience must have left her somewhat cynical, and she did not take the later proposals of royal suitors very seriously. The next to be turned down was her brother-in-law, Philip II of Spain. After him the Austrian Hapsburgs entered the lists. Their archives were recently opened in Vienna and revealed the most amazing reports of the envoys to England who for half a decade peddled the illustrious Archduke Charles to Elizabeth, with no success. She insisted that he should come to England to be inspected; they declared inspection impossible because if he came and was refused, it would mean a slight, which the illustrious archduke could not accept. While the argument over this question of eti-

*quette went on, the envoys wrote reports of enquiries concern-
ing the "maiden honor and integrity" of the queen, finding that
"all the aspersions against her are but spawn of envy, malice,
and hatred" and that the Earl of Leicester, her master of the
horse, was a "virtuous, pious, courteous, and highly moral
man whom the Queen loves as a brother, in most chaste and
honest love." In a special message the envoy implores the archduke to dress well and not to ride on hacks but to use the finest
palfreys because he had no doubt the queen would send secret
inspectors to see whether the archduke was as handsome as described. After eight years of such diplomatic courtship the persistent wooer sends this letter of proposal.*

 **Archduke Charles of Austria to
Queen Elizabeth of England**

VIENNA, OCTOBER 8, 1567

*I*llustrious Queen and Lady, Beloved and Vener-
ated Cousin, Greeting, All Happiness, and the Assurance of My Sincere and Unfailing Willingness to serve
you.

The Noble Earl of Sussex has delivered to us the much coveted letter from Your Highness, and then, as commanded orally and with much eloquence, set forth all that your Highness in your sincerity, affection, and kindness, intended for us. This afforded us much pleasure and solace. And though prior to this we had always been devoted to your Highness and studious of all that would be acceptable to you, this magnanimous and splendid proof of your good will has endeared you still more to us; and we candidly avow that we shall also in future endeavor to preserve for ourself this benevolence and to foster its growth; for we know nothing more agreeable and desirable than to adore your Highness with worthy thoughts, honors, and eulogies. . . .

As regards the negotiations themselves, which the noble Earl of Sussex is now conducting with His Imperial Majesty our liege-lord and brother in our affairs, we would not pester your Highness with verbose recapitulations, more especially as we do not doubt that the Earl will accomplish everything in entire concordance with Your Highness's wishes.

May it please your Highness, however, to learn from these lines that insofar as it is compatible with our conscientious belief, we shall in this present business endeavor to accommodate ourself to Your High-

ness's wishes, and besides in this as in all other matters be studious of your desires.

We are convinced that Your Highness as Queen
and Princess, endowed with clemency and courtesy
and distinguished with every kind of virtue, will with
the same special affection, answer us in kindness and
good will, and will be at all pains to comprehend that
we shall in all sincerity use our best endeavors to grat-
ify your Highness, and to demonstrate our zeal by
deeds, if Eternal and Merciful Heaven preserve us in
health and strength and bless our undertakings with
success.

We commend ourself to Your Highness as

YOUR MOST DEVOTED COUSIN
Charles, Arch-Duke of Austria

Christina, Queen of Sweden, daughter of the beloved king Gustaf II, wrote the following letter when she was eighteen; a brilliant, neurotic, learned, and strong-willed royal tomboy, she was crowned when nineteen and terminated the Thirty Years War when twenty-two—making peace against the passionate opposition of her chancellor Oxenstierna and of her whole militaristic cabinet.

Her cousin Karl Gustaf, more of a soldier than a lover, described as "ugly, dumpy, thickset, common," could not retain her affection. In the end, rather than marry him she handed him the crown of Sweden and ran off to Rome, where she lived and died as an adventurous exile.

 Queen Christina of Sweden to Prince Karl Gustaf

JANUARY 5, 1644

Beloved Cousin,

I see by your letter that you do not trust your thoughts to the pen. We may, however, correspond with all freedom, if you send me the key to a cipher, and compose your letters according to it, and change the seals, as I do with mine. Then the letters may be sent to your sister, the Princess Maria. You must take every precaution, for never were people here so much against us as now; but they shall never get their way, so long as you remain firm. They talk a great deal of the Elector of Brandenburg, but neither he nor any one in the world, however rich he be, shall ever alienate my heart from you. My love is so strong that it can only be overcome by death, and if, which God forbid, you should die before me, my heart shall remain dead for every other, and my mind and affection shall follow you to eternity, there to dwell with you.

Perhaps some will advise you to demand my hand openly; but I beseech you, by all that is holy, to have patience for some time, until you have acquired some reputation in the war, and until I have the crown on my head. I entreat you not to consider this time long, but to think of the old saying: "He does not wait too long who waits for something good." I hope, by God's blessing, that it is a good thing we both are waiting for.

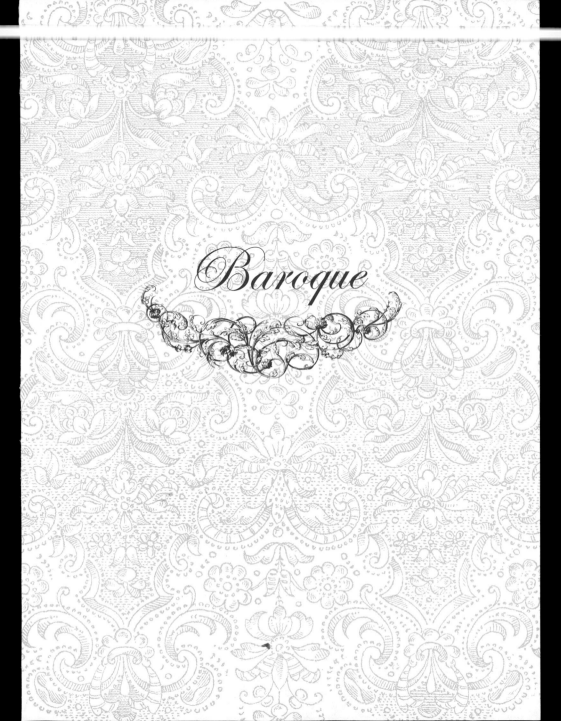

Baroque

Oliver Cromwell's youngest daughter, Frances—independent, modern-thinking, highly intelligent, brilliant—married, against her father's wishes, a grandson of the earl of Warwick, who left her a widow after five weeks. John Russell courted her in many letters, which she parried with all the smooth technique of an experienced heartbreaker. She surrendered in the end to become his wife.

 John Russell to Lady Frances Rich,
Countess of Warwick

   ABOUT 1662

*L*ove and fear, grief and impatience, are my perpetual tormentors. I cannot sleep but with a great deal of disturbance, I have not the same advantage of air as other men, I do not so much breathe as sigh. This is the condition I have been in ever since I saw you last, and now, Madam, that I have made known my torments to you, give me leave to tell you that there is nothing in this world can give me anything of ease but one line from your Ladyship, for which I as earnestly beg as I would for a morsel of bread if I were ready to starve; and since, Madam, it is in your power to take me off this rack, it concerns your generosity very much not to use cruelty to one who cries you quarter, and casts himself at your feet, where I beg that you would be pleased sometime that I am, Madam, your Ladyship's most humble and dutiful servant.

J. R.

Thomas Otway dedicated all the principal parts in his plays to Elizabeth Barry, the actress. She kept him in suspense for seven years. He died without winning her.

This letter was written at the time of the brilliant success of Otway's Venice Preserved, *which made him one of the first dramatists and her the first actress of their age.*

 Thomas Otway to Elizabeth Barry

 1682

*C*ould I see you without passion or be absent from you without pain, I need not beg your pardon for thus renewing my vows that I love you more than health, or any happiness here or hereafter. Everything you do is a new charm to me, and though I have languished for seven long years of desire, jealously despairing, yet every minute I see you I still discover something new and more bewitching. Consider how I love you; what would I not renounce and enterprize for you? I have you mine or I am miserable, and nothing but knowing which shall be the happy hour can make the rest of my years that are to come, tolerable. . . .

Remember poor Otway

John Hervey published the seventy letters that his father, Thomas Hervey, and his mother exchanged before they married. These were Attic in style. He himself, after the death of his first wife, fell in love with Elizabeth Felton, and after settling financial matters with her father, wrote to her in true Baroque.

 John Hervey to Elizabeth Felton

    JULY 20, 1695

My ever-new Delight,

The grateful goodness you have shown in bringing so much nicety of taste and natural indifferency as you are owner of to sett some little value upon a man whose greatest meritt is loving and thinking of you as he does, abates of the vanity might otherwise have been justly charg'd upon me in supposing that you should interess your self enough in what concerns me to care how I passd my journey; but the kind permission you allow'd me to take the pleasing liberty of writing to you being a further warrant and excuse for the trouble I am giving you, I will employ the happy priviledg to better purpose than acquainting you with my being well come to this place. Lett me bestow it in venting and doing justice to a heart full of love & faithfulness towards you. To tell you it is everything you coud wish it in your regard is not yet expressing rightly what it means and feels for you; no, saying it pays you by anticipation all that you can invent or expect or require from it, (were your demands unreasonable enough to be proportioned to the virtues which lay claim to it) would not come up to that degree of love and admiration Armida's charming prettynesses and touching decencies have created in it.

Thou'rt now become my thoughts perpetual theme,
Their daily longing and their nightly dream.

To please and make thee happy shall be the sole drift & constant meditation of my soul; and whenever I steal a moment's consideration that doth not tend directly and immediately to that end, 'tis how to make myself so in thee; in order whereunto I have been this night with Mr. Folkes, who hath promised to give the most expeditious turn to my affair that his witt can contrive; but saies it is not practicable by Tuesday; had it been so, my impatience to see thee again is such that even that day, so early as he may count it, would have been and is look'd upon as distant as doomsday to an expectation like mine. And now I have said this, lett me ask your pardon for the rest I broke you of the night before I died; (for is it not a death when soul and body separate?) But now I think on't, if that be a fault, no body is so criminal as yourself toward me; lett us then cry Quitts as to that matter; but I must observe, you could sleep when I was there present, which is more than he can do absent, who is, sleeping or waking, dead or living, worthy Armida's unworthy lover, friend and servant

J. H.

Rococo

Richard Steele, later coeditor of the Tatler *and the* Spectator, *left Cambridge University without a degree, to join the army. An impecunious but attractive captain, in 1705 he married a wealthy elderly widow, Mrs. Stretch, who died a year later. On the occasion of her funeral, he met Miss Mary Scurlock. In 1707 he married her secretly, perhaps to escape the charge of being too quickly consoled in his bereavement. "Dear Prue" tried to keep him out of debt but did not always succeed. She was genuinely attached to him and preserved all his letters, over four hundred. In them he calls her, before the wedding, his "charmer and inspirer"; afterwards, his "ruler and his absolute governess."*

Richard Steele to Mary Scurlock

　　　　　LORD SUNDERLAND'S OFFICE, 1707

Madam,

With what language shall I address my lovely fair, to acquaint her with the sentiments of an heart she delights to torture? I have not a minute's quiet out of your sight; and when I'm with you, you use me with so much distance that I am still in a state of absence, heightened with a view of the charms I am denied to approach. In a word, you must give me either a fan, a mask or a glove you have worn, or I cannot live; otherwise you must expect I'll kiss your hand, or, when I next sit by you, steal your handkerchief. You yourself are too great a bounty to be received at once; therefore I must be prepared by degree, lest the mighty gift distract me with joy. Dear Mrs. Scurlock, I am tir'd with calling you by that name; therefore say the day in which you will take that of, Madam,

YOUR MOST OBEDIENT,

MOST DEVOTED HUMBLE SERVANT

Richard Steele

*O*ne of the great ironists of the eighteenth century, Jonathan Swift, whose savage satire Gulliver's Travels *became, ironically, a juvenile best seller, had two abortive romances. Some biographers insist that he was secretly married to Esther Johnson, the "Stella" of his poems, though it is certain that Swift never lived with Stella. Another young girl, "Vanessa," spent her life yearning for Dean Swift's love, but when she found he would not marry her, she died of a broken heart—and consumption.*

This next letter is one of mock proposal, addressed to a married woman, Mrs. Howard, Lady of the Bedchamber to Queen Caroline. It refers to the severe headaches from which the lady suffered.

 Jonathan Swift to Mrs. Howard, Lady of the Bedchamber to Queen Caroline

 TWICKENHAM, AUGUST 14, 1727

*M*adam,

I wish I were a young lord and you were unmarried. I should make you the best husband in the world; for I am ten times deafer than you ever were in your life, and instead of a poor pain in the face I have good substantial giddiness and head-ache. The best of it is that though we might lay our heads together, you could tell me no secrets that might not be heard five rooms distant. These disorders of mine, if they hold as long as they used to do some years ago, will last as long as my license of absence—which I shall not renew, and then the Queen will have the misfortune not to see me, and I shall go back with the satisfaction never to have seen her since she was queen, but when I kissed her hands; and although she were a thousand queens, I will not lose my privilege of never seeing her but when she commands it.

I told my two landlords here that I would write you a love-letter, which I remembered you commanded me to do last year; but I would not show it to either of them. I am the greatest courtier and flatterer you have; because I try your good sense and taste more than all of them put together, which is the greatest compliment I could put upon you, and you have hitherto behaved yourself tolerably under it. . . . I will say another thing in your praise—that goodness would become you better than any other person I know, and for that very reason there is nobody I wish to be good as much as yourself.

I AM, EVER, WITH THE TRUEST RESPECT AND ESTEEM & &

Jonathan Swift

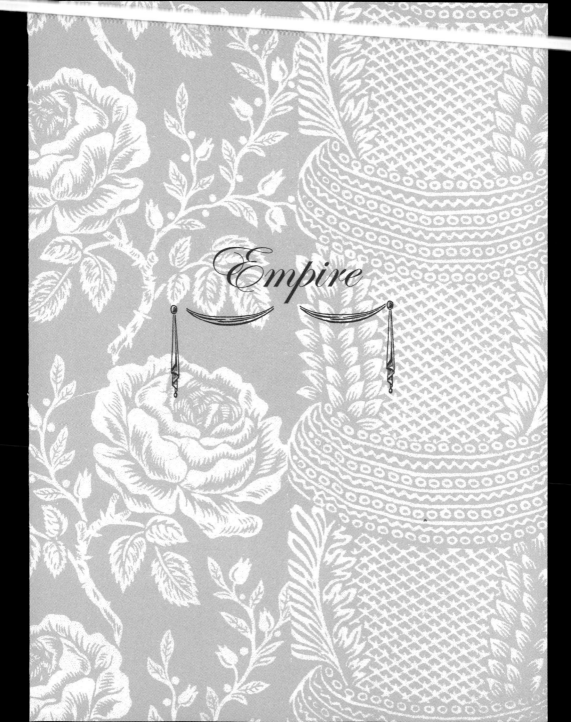

Empire

HE EIGHTEENTH CENTURY PRODUCED a male forerunner of Emily Post. He was fifty years old, a printer in a publishing firm. His employer suggested that he should write a manual of letters for "important family occasions," something in the line of the messages that Western Union offered to its clients. The manual was a success and the writer, incidentally, became the father of the modern English novel. His name was Samuel Richardson.

Everybody wrote letters now. The universal fashion rubbed off some of the individual charm of the earlier documents, In exchange for it there came a general fluency of language, which sometimes grew into formality and ended up in the rigid stiffness, coldness, and severity of the "Empire." The Empire style had its source in Napoleon's desire to revive the grandeur of the old Roman Empire. Its best presentation is Napoleon's own proposal letter to the archduchess Maria Louise of Austria.

L'Empire was eclectic in its combination of Renaissance, Byzantine, and Egyptian elements. Its metallic ornaments symbolize military rule of minds and bodies. It led up to the mixture of all possible and impossible styles characteristic of the Victorian age.

FROM SAMUEL RICHARDSON'S
Familiar Letters on Important Occasions

Hodge the Plowman to his Sweetheart Joan

 1741

Sweet Honey Joan,

I have sent thee a thing, such a one as the Gentle-folk call a love letter, it was indited by myself after I had drunk two or three pots of ale, but it was written in Roman joining hand by the schoolmaster who is clark of the parish, to whom I gave sixpence for his pains. Truly Joan, and Marry Joan, thou knowest how many a time and oft I have fetched home the cows when nobody knew who did it. Marry Joan, thou knowest I always played on thy side at Stool-Ball; and when thou didst turn the garland in the Whitsun holidays, I was sure to be drunk that night with joy. Marry Joan, cry I still, but wilt thou marry me, Joan? I know thou doest love Will the Taylor, who, it is true, is a very quiet man and foots it most fetuously; but I can tell thee, Joan, I think I shall be a better man than he very shortly, for I am learning of a fiddler to play on the kit, so that if you will not yield the sooner, I will ravish thee ere long with my music. Tis true I never

gave thee a token but I have here sent you one I bought
in the Exchange where all the folks hooted at me, but
thought I, hoot and be hanged an you will so I buy a
Top Knot for Joan; it will make a better show in church
than a green bay leaf by thy side. But what wilt thou
give me for that, Joan? Alas, I ask nothing but thyself;
come, Joan, give me thyself. Law ye what a happy day
that would be, to see thee with thy best clothes on, at
Church, and the Parson saying, I, Hodge, take thee
Joan, and by the Mass I would take thee and hug thee
and hug thee and buss thee, and then away to the Ale-
house and hey for the Musicianers and the Canaries
and the Sillybubs, and the Shoulder of Mutton and
Gravy; and so having no more to say, I rest assured of
your own good will

THY OWN DEAR SWEETHEART TRULY

Roger

James Boswell is better known by his Life of Johnson *than by his own life. The following letter is addressed to the daughter of a prominent Dutch family whom he met while studying in Utrecht. The girl turned him down. Who can blame her?*

 James Boswell to Isabella de Zuylen

 BERLIN, JULY 9, 1764

My dear Zelide,

Be not angry with me for not writing to my fair friend before now. You know I am a man of form, a man who says to himself, Thus will I act, and acts accordingly. In short, a man subjected to discipline, who has his *orders* for his conduct during the day with as much exactness as any soldier in any service. And who gives these orders? I give them. Boswell when cool and sedate fixes rules for Boswell to live by in the common course of life, when perhaps Boswell might be dissipated and forget the distinctions between right and wrong, between propriety and impropriety. I own to you that this method of living according to a plan may sometimes be inconvenient and may even cause me to err. When such a man as I am, employs his great judgment to regulate small matters, methinks he resembles a giant washing teacups or threading a needle, both of which operations would be much better performed by a pretty little miss. There now is a pompous affectation of dignity; you must expect a good deal of this from me; but you have indeed seen me often enough not to be surprised at it. . . . It was part of my system not to write to Zelide till my journey should be over. By my following that system, you must be almost four weeks without hearing a word from me. I will not pretend to doubt of your being sorry at this. I have even vanity enough to make me view you in tender attitudes of anxiety, such, however, as becomes a friend. Love is a passion which you and I have no thought of, at least for each other. . . . I am just a gentleman upon his travels, who has taken an attachment to you and who has your happiness at heart. I may add, a gentleman whom you honour with your esteem. My dear Zelide: You are very good, you are very candid. Pray, forgive me for begging you to be less vain. You have fine talents of one kind; but are you deficient in others? Do you think your *reason* is as distinguished as your imagination? Believe me, Zelide, it is not. Believe me and endeavour to improve. . . .

You tell me, "Je ne vaudrois rien pour votre femme, je n'ai pas les talents subalternes." If by these talents

you mean the domestic virtues you will find them nec-
essary for the wife of every sensible man. But there are
many stronger reasons against your being my wife;
so strong that, as I said to you formerly, I would not be
married to you to be a king. I know myself and I know
you. And from all probability of reasoning, I am very
certain that if we were married together, it would not
be long before we should both be very miserable. My
wife must have a character directly opposite to my
dear Zelide, except in affection, in honesty, and in
good humour. . . .

Defend yourself. Tell me that I am the severe Cato.
Tell me that you will make a very good wife. Let me
ask you then, Zelide, could you submit your inclina-
tions to the opinion, perhaps the *caprice* of a husband?
Could you do this with cheerfulness, without losing
any of your sweet good humour, without boasting of
it? Could you live quietly in the country six months of
the year? Could you make yourself agreeable to plain
honest neighbours? . . . Could you live thus and be
content, could you have a great deal of amusement in
your own family? Could you give spirits to your husband when he is melancholy? I have known such
wives, Zelide. What think you? Could you be such a
one? If you can, you may be happy with the sort of
man I once described to you. Adieu.

Laurence Sterne introduced into the language and into literature a new word—"sentimental"—which he used to describe a state of tender emotion with which he was especially familiar. He first used it in a letter to his future wife, Elizabeth Lumley, who eventually went insane because Sterne was "always miserably in love with someone outside of the domestic circle." While she was living in France, an invalid, he wrote to Eliza Draper, wife of an elderly government official in India home on a visit. She fell for the charm of the famous author.

 Laurence Sterne to Eliza Draper

 1767

I wish to God, Eliza, it was possible to postpone the voyage to India for another year— You owe much, I allow, to your husband; you owe something to your appearance and the opinion of the world; but trust me, my dear, you owe much likewise to yourself. . . . I will send for my wife and daughter and they shall carry you in pursuit of health to Montpellier, the wells of Bancois, the Spa or whither thou wilt. Thou shalt direct them and make parties of pleasure in what corner of the world fancy points out to thee. We shall fish upon the banks of Arno, and lose ourselves in the sweet labyrinths of its valleys. . . . Indeed I begin to think you have as many virtues as my uncle Toby's widow. Talking of widows—pray, Eliza, if ever you are such, do not think of giving yourself to some wealthy Nabob—because I design to marry you myself. My wife cannot live long—she has sold all the provinces in France already—I know not the woman I should like so well for her substitute as yourself. 'Tis true I am ninety-five in constitution, and you but twenty-five— rather too great a disparity this!—but what I want in youth I will make up in wit and good humor. Not Swift so loved his Stella, Scarron his Maintenon or Waller his Saccharissa, as I will love and sing thee, my wife elect! And those names, eminent as they were, shall give place to thine, Eliza. Tell me in answer to this that you approve and honor the proposal; and that you would (like the Spectator's mistress) have more joy in putting on an old man's slippers than associating with the gay, the voluptuous and the young.

ADIEU! BY SIMPLICIA!

YOURS

Tristram

*Friedrich Schiller, German poet, was for some time equally de-
voted to both the sisters Lengefeld, Karoline and Charlotte. He
could not make up his mind, till Karoline, the elder sister, made
up his mind for him and decided that he should marry Lotte,
the younger one. Three years after he had been introduced to
them, he married Lotte and they lived happily ever after.*

 Friedrich Schiller to Charlotte von Lengefeld

          LEIPZIG, AUGUST 3, 1789

*I*s it true, dearest Lotte? May I hope Caroline has
read in your soul and answered me from your heart
the question I did not dare to put myself? Oh, how
heavy this secret has become—I have kept it as long
as we know each other. Often, while we were living in
the same house, I came to you, resolved to reveal it to
you—but my courage left me. I thought I was selfish in
my desires . . . considering only my own happiness. . . . If I could not mean to you what you meant to
me, I might have destroyed the harmony of our friendship through my confession. And yet there were moments when my hopes rose again . . . when I even
thought it noble to bring you all the rest as a sacrifice.
You might be happy without me—you could never be

unhappy through me. You might give yourself to another, but none could love you more purely or tenderly than I. To no one could your happiness be more sacred than it was and always will be to me. I dedicate my very existence and everything in me, everything, my dearest, to you, and if I strive to make myself more noble, it is only to make myself more worthy of you, to make you happier. Our friendship and love will be indestructible and eternal, like the feelings on which they are based. . . .

Tell me that everything that Caroline let me hope is true. Tell me that you will be mine, and that my happiness will cost you no sacrifice. Oh! Assure me of this, and with but a single word. Our hearts have been neighbors for long. Let us break down that single partition that stands between us and let nothing stand between the free communication of our souls.

Farewell, my dearest Lotte. I long for a calm moment to describe to you all the feelings of my heart, which have made me so happy and again so unhappy, during the long time that this *one* longing has been in my soul. How much I still have to say!

Do not delay in banishing forever my unrest. I consign all the joys of my life to you. I can think of my joys under no other form than your image. Farewell, my dearest.

Schiller

Sir Walter Scott had been very much in love with a young girl who married someone else. His proposal to Charlotte Carpenter (Charpentier), the daughter of a French refugee, was accepted. She made him a good wife, but his affection for her was more of the rational than of the passionate sort. He took it out in his novels, where he put all the romance that life had denied him.

 Sir Walter Scott to Charlotte Carpenter

                    1797

Since Miss Carpenter has forbid my seeing her for the present, I am willing to incur even the hazard of her displeasure by intruding upon her in this manner. My anxiety, which is greater than I can find words to express, leads me to risque what I am sure if you could but know my present [condition] would not make you very, very angry.

Gladly would I have come to Carlisle to-morrow, and returned here to dinner; but dearly as I love my friend, I would ever sacrifice my own personal gratification to follow the line of conduct which is most agreeable to her. I likewise wish to enter more particularly into the circumstances of my situation, which I should most heartily despise myself were I capable of concealing or misrepresenting to you. Being only the second brother of a large family, you will easily conceive that tho' my father is a man in easy circumstances, my success in life must depend upon my own exertions. This I have been always taught to expect, and far from considering it as a hardship, my feelings on that subject have ever been those of confidence in myself.

Hitherto, from reasons which have long thrown a lassitude over my mind, to which it is not naturally liable, my professional exertions have been culpably neglected; and as I reside with my father, I gave myself little trouble, provided my private income did but answer my personal expense and the maintenance of a horse or two. At the same time, none of those who were called to the Bar with myself can boast of having very far outstripped me in the career of life or of business.

I have every reason to expect that the Sheriffdom of a particular County, presently occupied by a gentleman in a very precarious state of health, may soon fall to my lot. The salary is 250 pounds per annum, and the duty does not interfere with the exercise of my profession, but greatly advances it. . . . Many other little resources, which I cannot easily explain so as to make you comprehend me, induce me to express myself with confidence upon the probability of my success; and oh, how dear these prospects will become to me would my beloved friend but permit me to think that she would share them!

If you could form any idea of the society in Edinburgh, I am sure the prospect of living there would not terrify you. Your situation would entitle you to take as great a share in the amusements of the place as you were disposed to; and when you were tired of these, it should be the study of my life to prevent your feeling one moment's *Ennui*. When care comes, we will laugh it away; or if the load is too heavy, we will sit down and share it between us, till it becomes almost as light as pleasure itself. You are apprehensive of losing your liberty; but could you but think with how many domestic pleasures the sacrifice will be repaid, you would no longer think it very frightful. Indisposition may deprive you of that liberty which you prize so highly, and age certainly will. Oh, think how much happier you will find yourself, surrounded by friends who will love you, than with those who will only regard even my beloved Charlotte while she possesses the power of interesting or entertaining them.

You seem, too, to doubt the strength, or at least the stability, of my affection; I can only protest to you most solemnly that a truer never warmed a mortal's breast, and that though it may appear sudden it is not rashly adopted. You yourself must allow that from the nature of our acquaintance, we are entitled to judge more absolutely of each other, than from a much longer one trammelled with the usual forms of life; and tho' I have been repeatedly in similar situations with amiable and accomplished women, the feelings I entertain for you have ever been strangers to my bosom, except during a period I have often alluded to.

I have settled in my mind to see you on Monday next. I stay thus long to give you time to make what inquiries you may think proper, and also because you seemed to wish it. All Westmoreland and Cumberland shall not detain me a minute longer. In the meanwhile I do not expect you to write. You shall do nothing to commit yourself. How this week will pass away I know not; but a more restless, anxious being never numbered the hours than I have been this whole day. Do not think of bidding me *forget you*, when we again meet— Oh, do not; the thing is really impossible, as impossible as it is to express how much I love you, and how truly I believe our hearts were formed for each other. Mr. and Mrs. B. are Hospitality itself, but all will not do. I would fain make you laugh before concluding, but my heart is rather too full for trifling. Adieu, adieu, souvenez-vous de moi.

W. Scott

Gebhard Leberecht von Blücher, the German field marshal who, with Wellington, conquered Napoleon, had lost his wife in 1791 and proposed to the very wealthy Frau von S., as follows, in March 1795. But on April 1 he withdrew his proposal "because of too unequal fortunes." He later married a girl thirty years younger than he, Amalie von Colomb, and was very happy with her.

 Field Marshal von Blücher to Frau von S.

     1795

Most gracious lady!

I acknowledge the sentiments which you have expressed for me, gratefully and respectfully. My silence is unpardonable, but I am too honorable and it is just this which justifies my conduct. I have never yet deceived anyone; I should like least of all to deceive you. Well, to business!

1. How can I ask you to marry me, when all my affairs are topsy-turvy, and I am in debt to the extent of 5,000 dollars? To be sure, my prospects are good; I have a good job which can support me fairly well. But we cannot count on its permanence.

2. I have three children whom I love. Their mother made me her heir but I gave up the inheritance in favor of my beloved children. My children are well taken care of, but I have nothing.

3. I am not much of a hand at saving money. Living with my officers, helping my subalterns when they need money—this makes me happy. But I cannot get rich at it.

4. I can't enter upon any marriage which does not make provision for my old age and for the welfare of my children. Please understand me correctly; I am a long way from asking that the lady who grants me her hand in marriage should also turn over to me her income for the rest of her life; far from it! But your income will have to be added to mine, so that I may be in a position to maintain my social standing, character, and wife properly. I am aware, dear lady, that you are the possessor of a considerable income; your feelings for me are tender; your magnanimity cannot exceed my gratitude. Well then! If you are resolved to make me happy—my hand and heart are at your feet. If, as I

sincerely hope, you outlive me, do not count on my leaving any wealth behind, because I possess none.

Dear Lady, you have here my frank and honest confession of faith; treat me in a similar manner! Tell me what you intend to do for me. I will take infinite pains to deserve your love and friendship, and will always strive to keep you from regretting your decision to marry me. There is just one more thing I must mention: I have a daughter ten years of age, whom I idolize. I shall give this child into your arms and humbly beseech you to watch over her rearing, since you yourself already have the perfection that I should like to see her attain. . . .

Honor me with a speedy answer! Let me know where I stand! And count on the unbounded respect of him who loves and honors you

Blücher

Napoleon Bonaparte's proposal to the archduchess of Austria is very Empire. Ten years earlier he had written Baroque letters of passion to Josephine, but he needed a son for succession, and so, at the peak of his power, he divorced her and was accepted by the Hapsburg princess. She did not love him, but she gave him the heir to the crown, who bore the title of a "king of Rome." When Napoleon was exiled, she attached herself to the Count Neipperg, whom she married after Napoleon's death in 1821. The son died as a young boy.

 Emperor Napoleon I to
Archduchess Maria Louise of Austria

RAMBOUILLET, FEBRUARY 23, 1810

Dear Cousin,

The striking qualities which enhance your person have inspired in us the desire to serve and honor you.

We are requesting the Emperor, your respected father, to entrust to us the happiness of Your Imperial Highness.

May we be permitted to hope that you will receive graciously the feelings which impel us to take this step? May we harbor the flattering hope that you will agree to this marriage not only because of filial obedience and duty?

If Your Imperial Highness has but the slightest affection for us, we will cultivate this feeling with the greatest pains, and make it our supreme task ever to seek your happiness in every respect. In this way we fondly hope to win your complete affection some day. That is our most fervent wish, and we beg Your Imperial Highness to be favorably inclined to us.

Napoleon

Augustus Frederick, Duke of Sussex, sixth son of George III, far enough from succession to the throne, was happier than other princes in that he could marry a commoner without upsetting world affairs. He had met Lady Augusta Murray in Rome. She was six years older than he and refused his first proposals in his own interest, but he persisted, got hold of Mr. Gunn, a minister of the Church of England resident in Rome, made him promise to perform the marriage ceremony, and went on a hunger strike as shown by his letter. It proved successful.

 Augustus Frederick, Duke of Sussex, to Lady Augusta Murray

 ROME, 1820

*W*ill you allow me to come this evening? It is my only hope. Oh let me come and we will send for Mr. Gunn. Everything but this is hateful to me. More than forty-eight hours have passed without my taking the smallest nourishment. Oh let me not live so. Death is certainly better than this—which if in forty-eight hours it has not occurred must follow; for by all that is holy, till I am married I will eat nothing, and if I am not married the promise will die with me. I am resolute. Nothing shall alter my resolution. If Gunn will not marry me I shall die. . . .

Prince William of Prussia, who, with Bismarck as his chancellor, later united, as William I, the quibbling tribes of Northern Europe into the German Reich, had been passionately in love with Princess Elizabeth Radziwill, but he had to give her up because the king, his father, put his foot down and said no. His letter to the Weimarian princess is in Empire style, and their relations, when they married, were of the same cool and formal kind. But she was a good empress and played her part as best she could.

**Prince William of Prussia to
Princess Augusta of Saxe-Weimar**

                 BERLIN, AUGUST 1828

I can scarcely describe to Your Highness the excitement which fills my heart at this moment when I take my pen in hand to make the most important move of my life.

With trepidation, but also with the assurance that God will be near me in this decisive moment, I approach you with confidence.

Your Highness herself has inspired this feeling of confidence in me, but many other feelings are closely connected with this one to make you inexpressibly dear to me and to bind me to you forever—if Your Highness will grant me your gracious consent. To learn whether I may expect this consent, whether I may see my fondest wishes fulfilled and count on a response to those feelings—to settle the uncertainty in my heart, may I expect Your Highness's decision and answer?

If my heart has not deceived me, I may receive from you a confirmation of my hopes. If God grants me his favor, I shall hasten, grateful to him and to you, to lay my gratitude at your feet in person.

I SIGN MYSELF AS
YOUR HIGHNESS'S MOST DEVOTED SERVANT
Wilhelm, Prince of Prussia

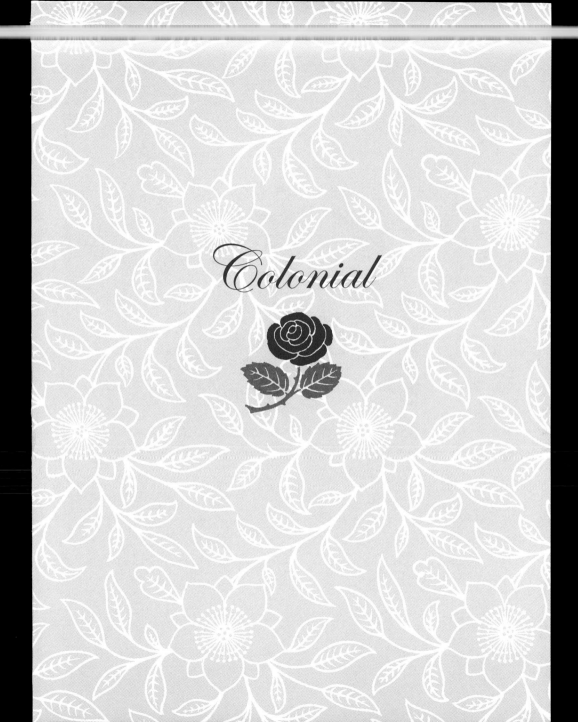

Colonial

*T*HE DISCOVERY OF A NEW WORLD and of the simple life as a religious experience is mirrored in the proposals of the early colonists in America. Colonial houses saw short widowhoods; widowers remarried as quickly as they could get mates. The scarcity of women allowed these to pick and choose, in log cabins as well as in plantation mansions.

The diaries of pious men are delicious proof of how eagerly they obeyed the Lord (who did not mean them to "lead a widower's life") and their own amorous impulses.

Girls often took the lead—like clever Betsy Hanford of Virginia. The reverend John Call, who had baptized her, was asked by one of her suitors to use his influence to impress upon her the Christian duty of marrying. The reverend talked to Betsy and did his best to make her accept the unsuccessful suitor. She accepted the principle but not the object. Pressed for reasons, she told the minister he would find the motive for her refusal in the Bible. She asked him to look up 2 Samuel 12:7. Returning to his study, he turned to the chapter and verse and saw these words:

Thou art the man.

A few months later a notice in the *Virginia Gazette* announced the marriage of the Reverend Call to Betsy Hanford.

Samuel Sewall, colonist, minister, judge in the Salem witch trials, was one of those full-blooded Puritans who loved life, enjoyed good food, and knew how to drive a bargain. He married three times, always putting the responsibility on the Lord. His famous diary describes his courtships after the death of his first wife, Judith Hull, who had borne him thirteen children. The widow Winthrop advises him to buy a new wig. Mrs. Denison tells him to procure another and better nurse. Whereupon he writes in his diary, "My bowels yearn towards the widow Denison; but I think God directs me in his providens to desist." The widow Tilly is willing; at the age of sixty-five, he marries her, but she falls sick on the wedding night and leaves him a widower again after half a year. Still undaunted in spirit he writes, at seventy, to the widow Gibbs and is accepted. They were married in March 1722.

Samuel Sewall to the widow Gibbs

JANUARY 12, 1722

Madam,

Your Removal out of Town, and the Severity of the Winter, are the reason of my making you this Epistolary Visit. In times past (as I remember) you were minded that I should marry you, by giving you to your desirable Bridegroom. Some sense of this intended Respect abides with me still; and puts me upon enquiring whether you be willing that I should Marry you now, by becoming your Husband; Aged, and feeble, and exhausted as I am, your favourable Answer to this Enquiry, in a few Lines, the Candor of it will much oblige, Madam, your humble Serv*ᵗ*

S. S.

This is the shortest proposal letter written before the twentieth century. It got results; S. P. was accepted.

 Samuel Parr to Jane Morsingale

 UNDATED

*M*adam, You are a very charming woman, and I should be happy to obtain you as a wife. If you accept my proposal I will tell you who was the author of Junius.

S. P.

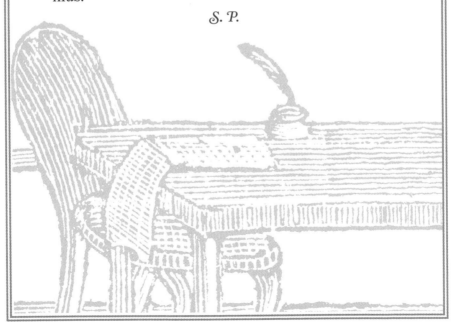

This is typical of the colonial proposals. They were nearly always directed to the parent; the children had not much say in the matter. They were, as a seventeenth-century manual on the **Duty of Man** *held it, so much the property of their parents, that to give themselves away without consent would have been called theft.*

 Thomas Walker to Jeremiah Moore

 1760s

Dear Sir,

My son, Mr. John Walker, having informed me of his intention to pay his addresses to your daughter Elizabeth, if he should be agreeable to yourself, lady and daughter, it may not be amiss to inform you what I feel myself able to afford for their support, in case of a union. My affairs are in an uncertain state, but I will promise one thousand pounds, to be paid in 1766, and the further sum of two thousands pounds I promised to give him; but the uncertainty of my present affairs prevents my fixing on a time of a payment. The above sums are all to be in money or lands and other effects at the option of my son, John Walker.

Thomas Walker

Abraham Lincoln, as a young clerk in a Salem store, had fallen in love with Anne Rutledge, the daughter of his landlord. When she died of malaria, a nervous depression clouded his life.

He then moved to Springfield and formed a new attachment. The object was Mary Owens, a "bouncing, sensible lass." The letter of proposal written to her is highly unusual. She turned him down.

Two years later he found himself engaged to Mary Todd, a beautiful girl of high spirits and higher social origin than he. The wedding day was set, everything prepared, the guests waiting, but he either forgot to turn up in church or failed in some other blatant way. A scandal flared up which was never quite explained. The engagement was broken off in January 1841, but there was a reconciliation a year later, and they were married in November 1842.

Abraham Lincoln to Mary Owens

 SPRINGFIELD, ILLINOIS, MAY 7, 1837

Friend Mary:

I have commenced two letters to send you before this, both of which displeased me before I got half done and so I tore them up. The first I thought was not serious enough, and the second was on the other extreme. I shall send this, turn out as it may.

This thing of living in Springfield is rather a dull business, after all; at least it is so to me. I am quite as lonesome here as I ever was anywhere in my life. I have been spoken to by but one woman since I have been here, and should not have been by her if she could have avoided it. I've never been to church yet, and probably shall not be soon. I stay away because I am conscious I should not know how to behave myself.

I am often thinking of what we said about your coming to live at Springfield. I am afraid you would not be satisfied. There is a great deal of flourishing about in carriages here, which it would be your doom to see without sharing it. You would have to be poor, without the means of hiding your poverty. Do you believe you could bear that patiently? Whatever woman may cast her lot with mine, should any ever do so, it is my intention to do all in my power to make her happy and contented; and there is nothing I can imagine that would make me more unhappy than to fail in the effort. I know I should be much happier with you than the way I am, provided I saw no signs of discontent in you. What you have said to me may have been in the way of jest, or I may have misunderstood it. If so, then let it be forgotten; if otherwise, I much wish you would think seriously before you decide. What I have said I will most positively abide by. My opinion is that you had better not do it. You have not been accustomed to hardship, and it may be more severe than you now imagine. I know you are capable of thinking correctly on any subject, and if you deliberate maturely upon this before you decide, then I am willing to abide by your decision.

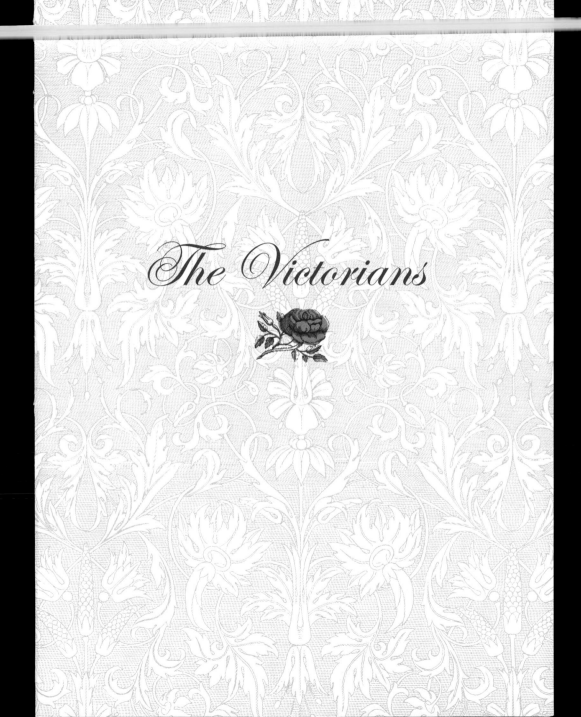

The Victorians

THE VICTORIAN AGE WAS ECLECTIC in its mixture of styles and in its constant swing of the pendulum between understatement and over-statement. It yields more proposal letters than any other age. Most of them are long and wordy. A small choice of them will show the trend.

William Hazlitt, famous essayist, started his career as a painter and became a friend of the Lake Poets Coleridge and Wordsworth. He wooed Sarah Stoddart, Mary Lamb's friend, in very simple language.

They married, but Hazlitt seems to have been a better essayist than husband. They were divorced in 1822. Two years later he married Mrs. Bridgewater. This second union did not last beyond a year's travel on the continent.

 William Hazlitt to Sarah Stoddart

 1808

...*I* would not give a pin for a girl whose cheeks never tingle—nor for myself if I could not make them tingle, sometimes. Now, though I always am writing to you about "lips and noses" and such sort of stuff, yet as I sit by my fireside (which I generally do eight or ten hours a day) I often think of you in a more serious and sober light. For indeed I never love you so well as when I think of sitting with you to dinner on a broiled scragg-end of mutton and hot potatoes. You then please my fancy more than when I think of you in . . . no, you would never forgive me if I were to finish the sentence. Now I think of it, what do you mean to be dressed in when we are married? But it does not much matter. I wish you would let your hair grow; though perhaps nothing will be better than "the same air and look with which at first my heart was took."

Charles Lamb, essayist, famous through the Tales from Shakespeare, *which he wrote with his sister Mary, proposed, late in life, to the actress Fanny Kelly.*

She said no—she was in love with someone else—but they remained friends.

 Charles Lamb to Fanny Kelly

 1819

Dear Miss Kelly,

We had the pleasure, pain I might better call it, of seeing you last night in the new play. It was a most consummate piece of acting, but what a task for you to undergo, at a time when your heart is sore with real sorrow. It has given rise to a train of thinking which I cannot suppress.

Would to God you were released from this way of life—that you could bring your mind to consent to take your lot with us, and throw off for ever the whole burden of your profession. . . . I neither expect nor wish you to take notice of that which I am writing in your present over-occupied and hurried state, but to think of it at your leisure. I have quite income enough, if that were all, to justify my making a proposal, with what I may call even a handsome provision for my survivor. What you possess of your own would naturally be apportioned to those for whose sakes chiefly you have made so many hard sacrifices. I am not so foolish as not to know that I am a most unworthy match for such a one as you, but you have for years been a principal object of my mind. In many a sweet assumed character have I learned to love you, but simply as F. M. Kelly I love you better than them all. Can you quit these shadows of existence and come and be reality to us? Can you leave off harassing yourself to please a thankless multitude who knows nothing of you, and begin at last to live for yourself and your friends?

IN HASTE, BUT WITH ENTIRE RESPECT
AND DEEPEST AFFECTION
Charles Lamb

The great composer Robert Schumann, when studying music in Leipzig with Friedrich Wieck, the pianist, came to an affectionate understanding with his teacher's daughter Clara. His proposal was turned down because of his uncertain future. After taking his degree, he married the girl against her father's will. Sixteen years later he died insane; Clara lived forty years longer and helped Johannes Brahms through years of a devoted friendship.

 Robert Schumann to Friedrich Wieck, for his daughter Clara

 SEPTEMBER 13, 1837

*W*hat I have to say to you is so simple—and yet the right words won't come. A trembling hand cannot guide a pen calmly. If I make some mistakes in grammar or expression, I beg your indulgence.

Today is Clara's birthday—the day on which the dearest thing on earth to me and to you first saw the light of this world. . . . If I say so myself, I have never viewed my future prospects so calmly as I do today. Securely fixed against need, so far as my human understanding can predict, ambitious ideas in my head, a heart moved to enthusiasm by everything noble, hands ready for work, conscious of the great effect I shall have, and still hopeful of doing everything that can be expected of my powers, honored and loved by many—I should think that would be enough! Oh! the painful answer I must give myself! What is all that, compared to the pain of being separated from the one being who makes all this striving worthwhile, and who returns my love truly and ardently. You know this being, you happy father, only too well. Ask her eyes if I have spoken the truth!

You tested me for eighteen months, as rigorously as Fate itself. I hurt you deeply, but you have let me atone for it. Now test me again as long. Perhaps, if you do not demand the impossible, my powers will keep pace with your desires; perhaps I shall gain your confidence again. You know I am persistent in matters of importance. If you find me capable, then bless this union of two souls, for whose greatest happiness nothing is lacking but parental blessing. It is not the excitement of the moment, not passion, nothing superficial that binds me to Clara with all the fibers of my being. It is the deep conviction that no marriage has ever been prepared under such a favorable harmony of circumstances; it is this adorable girl herself who radiates happiness and who guarantees ours. If you are also convinced of this, then give me a definite promise that for the time being you will decide nothing about Clara's future, as I give you my word not to speak to Clara against your wishes. Grant us just one thing, that when you go on lengthy trips, we may keep each other informed. . . .

With the deepest emotion of which an oppressed, loving heart is capable, I implore you: Give us your blessing, be once more a friend to one of your oldest friends, and to the best child in the world be the best father!

Robert Schumann

Otto von Bismarck, the "wild Junker," wrote this amazing letter to the pietist Puttkamer. Johanna became, as his wife, the symbol of the German hausfrau; she gave him a happy home life and the calm relaxation that his demonic temperament needed. That the future Iron Chancellor of the German Reich should have looked upon his early life in the way he makes out in his letter will be a revelation to those who idolize his memory as well as to those who hate what he stood for.

 Prince Otto von Bismarck to Herr von Puttkamer, for his daughter Johanna

 1846

*M*ost honored Herr von Puttkamer!

I begin this letter by indicating its contents; it is to ask you for the supreme thing that you can give away in this world: the hand of your daughter. I know I seem audacious if, known to you only recently and from sparse meetings, I ask you for the highest proof of trust that you can give to a man. I also know that, apart from all handicaps of space and time which might make it difficult for you to form an opinion of me, I shall by myself never be able to give you such security for the future as would warrant the handing over of such a precious pledge, unless you complete by faith in God what faith in man cannot do. What I can do is limited to my giving you information about myself with unreserved openness, so far as I have reached clarity about myself. You can easily get reports about my outward behavior from others; therefore I shall only give a description of my inner life, which is its base, and especially about my attitude towards Christianity.

I must go far back. I had early become a stranger to my parents' home and never felt completely at home there afterwards, and my education was carried out with a view to developing first and foremost practical reasoning and to submitting everything else to the acquisition of practical knowledge as early as possible. After irregularly attended and uncomprehended religious instruction I was confirmed by Schleirmacher on my sixteenth birthday; I had at that time no other religion except a naked deism, which did not remain long without an admixture of pantheism. It was about this time that I stopped saying my evening prayer as I had been accustomed to do from childhood; for praying seemed to me to be in contradiction to my view of God, who either by Himself, according to His omnipresence, was producing all my thoughts and my will—and, therefore, was praying through me to Himself—or if my will was independent of God's will, it would be presumptuous and indicate doubt in God's eternal constancy and the unchangeable completeness of His decisions if one tried to influence Him by prayer. Not quite seventeen, I went to the University of Gottingen. For eight years I rarely saw my parents' house. My father leniently left me alone; my mother, from a distance, rebuked me if I neglected my studies and professional work and obviously thought she could leave the rest to higher guidance. Apart from this the teaching and advice from others did not reach me. If in this period studies which ambition at times drove me to, or disgust with the emptiness of my life, brought me into contact with serious life and eternity, I looked into the philosophies of the ancients, or Hegel's half-understood writings, but first and foremost the mathematical clarity of Spinoza for reassurance about what human reason cannot grasp. To intensive thinking about this I only came through solitude when, after my mother's death six or seven years ago, I moved to Kniephof. Though my views did not change materially there in the beginning, an inner voice soon began to be audible in the solitude and to show me many things as wrong which I had thought permissible before. But always my endeavor towards understanding remained bound by the circle of reason, and led me through the reading of Strauss, Feuerbach, Bruno, Bauer, only deeper into the dead-end path of doubt. I came to the conclusion that God has denied man the possibility of understanding and that it was arrogance to pretend to know the will and the way of the Lord; that man must await in devotion what his Creator would decide about him in death, and that His will cannot be known to us on earth except through the voice of our conscience, which He has given us as a cornucopia through the darkness of the world. That I did not find peace in this faith I need not say; I passed many hours of disconsolate depression in the thought that my own and other people's existence was without aim and use, perhaps just a chance by-product of creation, coming and going, like dust rolling off the wheels.

Four years ago I met, for the first time since my school days, Moritz Blankenburg and found in him what I had never before had in my life: a friend; the warm zeal of his love tried in vain to give me, in discussions and talks, what I lacked: faith. But in his circle I found people who made me feel ashamed because I had tried with the poor light of my reason to probe into things which superior minds had accepted as true and sacred in childlike faith. I saw the members of this circle to be in their outward actions almost invariably examples of what I wished to be. I was not surprised to see that they had peace and trust, because I had never doubted that peace and trust were companions of faith; but faith cannot be given or taken—I felt I should have to wait to see whether it would come to me. But I felt happy in this circle with a happiness never felt before; I had a family to which I belonged, almost a home. . . .

I came, through others and by my own urge, to read the Bible, and what stirred in me came to life when our dear late friend in Cardemin fell fatally ill. My first prayer since childhood days was for her, and though God has not granted it, He has not turned it down, for I have not lost again the capacity for asking Him, and I feel, if not peace, faith and courage for life as I for long had not known it.

I do not know how you will value these feelings only two months old, but I hope I shall not lose them whatever shall be decided about my proposal, a hope which I could not assure you of otherwise than by my complete frankness and loyalty in what I have told you and nobody else, in the faith that God gives success to the loyal.

I refrain from every expression of feeling and intention as regards your daughter, for the step I am undertaking talks louder and more eloquently than words. Neither can promises for the future be of any use, for you know better than I the unreliability of the human heart. The only security for your daughter's welfare lies in my prayer for the blessing of the Lord. Historically I want to state that after I had seen Miss Johanna repeatedly in Cardemin, after our trip together this summer, I was only in doubt whether the fulfillment of my wishes would be in harmony with the happiness and peace of your daughter, and whether my self-confidence were not greater than my power if I thought I possessed the qualities she was entitled to find in a husband. Recently, with my trust in God's grace, the decision has matured in me which I now carry through; I have been silent in Zimmerhausen only because I had more to say than I could say by word of mouth. . . .

I am sure there is much which I have not said or not made clear enough in this letter; I am prepared, of course, to give precise and honest information about everything you would want to know. The most important things I believe I have said.

Please give your wife my devoted regards and accept the assurance of my love and respect with kindness.

Bismarck

Thomas Carlyle was no match for Jane Welsh; she was young, beautiful, and rich; he was a poor, highly nervous, and erratic genius and lacked all the essential qualities for a good husband. Her mother was opposed to the marriage. The couple corresponded for years. Jane herself was an excellent translator of folklore and a writer of distinction whose work Carlyle much admired, even at the peak of his own fame. In the end Jane decided to become a poor man's wife. She settled her fortune on her mother and married him. Their life together was one hurricane of happiness and misery, their home in Chelsea, with all its material discomforts and spiritual luxuries, was a center for the intellectual life of London at the time.

 Thomas Carlyle to Jane Welsh

 1823

My dear Jane,

I have longed for the arrival of this day . . . your letter was waiting for me, to welcome me. And such a welcome! I felt in reading it and reading it again as if it were more to me than the charter to all the metal of Potosi. What a frank and true and noble spirit is my Jane's! No artifice, no vulgar management; her sentiments come warm and fearless from her heart because they are pure and honest as herself, and the friend whom she trusts she trusts without reserve. I often ask myself: Is not all this a dream? Is it true that the most enchanting creature I have ever seen does actually love me? No! Thank God it is not a dream; Jane loves me! She loves me! and I swear by the Immortal Powers that she shall yet be mine, as I am hers, through life and death and all the dark vicissitudes that wait us here and hereafter. In more reasonable moments I perceive that I am very selfish and almost mad. Alas! My fate is dreary and perilous and obscure; is it fit that you whom I honour among the fairest of God's works, whom I love more dearly than my own soul, should partake of it? . . . If I were intellectual sovereign of all the world, if I were—but it is vain to speculate. I know that I am nothing. I know not that I shall not always be so. The only thing I know is that you are the most delightful, enthusiastic, contemptuous, capricious, affectionate, sarcastic, warmhearted, lofty-minded half-devil, half-angel of a woman that ever ruled over the heart of a man; that I will love you, must love you, whatever betide, till the last moment of my existence, and that if we both act rightly our lot *may* be the happiest of a thousand mortal lots. So let us cling to one another (if you dare, if thus forewarned)—forever and ever! . . . You will yet be blessed yourself in making me more blessed than man has right to look for being upon earth. God bless you, my heart's darling!

Victor Hugo, who in his later life scarcely could have been called Victorian, exhibited some of the style of his namesake on the British throne in his early lovemaking. His young fiancée, Adele Faucher, had offered to live with him, should his father refuse to permit their marriage. She preferred living in sin to having her boyfriend go crazy as his brother Eugene did. His letter was written while he was waiting for his father's permission. They were married, and Eugene, also in love with Adele, went to the madhouse and died there. Victor became rich, famous, and highly influential in the political life of France, but the harmony of his married life was disturbed by his amorous escapades, which often proved more sensational, dramatic, and fantastic than even his plays and novels.

 Victor Hugo to Adele Faucher

 1822

*A*dele, to what follies, to what delirium did not your Victor give way ... sometimes I was ready to accept your offer; ... I thought we would go across France ... by day we would travel in the same carriage, by night sleep under the same roof. But do not think, my noble Adele, that I would have taken advantage of so much happiness . . . you would have been the object of the most worthy respect . . . you might on the journey even have slept in the same chamber without fearing that I would have alarmed you by a touch or have even looked at you. I would have slept, or watched wakefully, on a chair or lying on the floor beside your bed, the guardian of your repose, the protector of your slumbers.

The letter of proposal, not for marriage, that the Austrian playwright Johann Nestroy wrote to a lady of light reputation has found a place here because it is unique. The writer did not sign his real name; he added "von" to his pseudonym, to appear to be of the nobility, because he probably presumed that might impress the lady more than his other "attractions."

 Johann Nestroy to Fräulein Koefer

MARCH 12, 1855

 To Fräulein von Koefer,
Stadt, Schultergasse 402
on the third floor

Mein Fräulein!

Not only this letter in itself, but also its length will amaze you (I risk it, as I risk its complete lack of success). I will not tire your patience by the usual lengthy excuses but come straight to the point.

I never spend an evening without going to the theater. Therefore I have seen you repeatedly. I do not think I was happy enough to be noticed by you—one is generally unnoticed if one presents oneself with one's missus, chained in marriage (though perhaps otherwise not without attractions). One time a couple of dandies, in the second box from mine, were the aim of your opera glasses and the subject of my secret envy.

I dare express in these lines what you must have heard from others, and often: that you are in the highest degree attractive, interesting, and the object of my most passionate desires.

How are you going to take these words? Maybe you will laugh at me as an impudent, unknown man. Maybe if you have a lover—and it is almost unthinkable that you should not have one—you will laugh at me with him. Then I can console myself with the thought that you might not have laughed had you known me.

I do not know your conditions of life. I have most strictly forbidden my manservant who followed you going home and found out your name from a fellow standing on the stairs (he was very unfriendly) every further curiosity which might have hurt your feelings if you had heard about it. My opinion is: beautiful young ladies in whatever circumstances of life ought not to turn down a discreet friend made secretly happy and immensely grateful. Even if you should be engaged to be married, such a secret friend might not be without use to you after the honeymoon. If you agree, I hope you will not refuse my proposal. . . .

I shall choose a harmless hour—two o'clock in the afternoon—and a harmless location—the main avenue in the Prater. Tomorrow at half past one I shall be riding from the lower end of the avenue to its upper end, the Praterstern. If you, at the same time, will ride from the Praterstern to the Rondeau, our carriages will pass each other. Please hold your handkerchief out of the right window of your carriage (seeing we drive on the left in Vienna) so that I can recognize your carriage from a distance. This handkerchief will be the thrilling sign for me that, in case you find me worthy of your affection, you will agree to my views as expressed above about a secret liaison.

As many carriages pass the Corso at this time, I shall make myself known to you by a light gray traveling coat piped with red. I shall not attempt to follow you, but I will take your appearance as permission for the next step which I am going to take. That will be another letter, which you will receive on the following day (Friday). In that I shall propose the place and time where we shall meet and talk with each other . . . I should suggest next Sunday as the day.

YOUR DEVOTED ADMIRER

L. B. von R.

Leo Nikolayevich Tolstoy, great Russian poet and life reformer, as a mature man lost his heart to Sofia Behrs, daughter of a physician. He was visiting them, and he could never muster courage to talk to her. The family thought he was in love with her elder sister, till he, in this intense, shy, and almost hysterical way, proposed. She accepted him. Their married life was an adventure of storms and revolutions up to the moment when he, an old man, left his home to go and die in complete solitude.

 Count Leo Tolstoy to Sofia Behrs

 1862

Sofia Andreyevna, it is becoming unbearable. For three weeks I've been saying to myself, "I shall tell her now," and yet I continue to go away with the same feeling of sadness, regret, terror, and happiness in my heart. Every night I go over the past and curse myself for not having spoken to you, and wonder what I would have said if I *had* spoken. I am taking this letter with me, in order to hand it to you should my

courage fail me again. Your family have the false no-
tion, I believe, that I am in love with Lisa. This is quite
wrong. Your story has clung to my mind because, after
reading it, I have come to the conclusion that "Prince
Dublitzky" has no right to think of happiness, and
that your poetic view of love is different . . . that I am
not jealous, and must not be jealous, of the man you
will love. I thought I could love you all like children. I
wrote at Ivitsy, "Your presence reminds me too vividly
of my old age"—*your* presence in particular. But then,
as now, I was lying to myself. At Ivitsy I might still
have been able to break away and to return to my her-
mitage, back to my solitary work and my absorbing
labors. Now I can't do anything; I feel I have created a
disturbance in your home, and that your friendship
for me, as a good, honorable man, has also been
spoiled. I dare not leave and I dare not stay. You are a
candid, honest girl; with your hand on your heart, and
without hurrying (for God's sake, don't hurry!), tell
me what to do. I would have laughed myself sick a
month ago if I had been told that I would suffer, suffer joyfully, as I have been doing for this past month.
Tell me, with all the candor that is yours: Will you be
my wife? If you can say *yes, boldly,* with all your heart,
then *say it;* but if you have the faintest shadow of
doubt, say *no.* For heaven's sake, think it over care-

fully. I am terrified to think of a *no*, but I am prepared for it and will be strong enough to bear it. But it will be terrible if I am not loved by my wife as much as I love you!

Anton Bruckner, Austrian composer of beautiful symphonies, was shy and clumsy in everything but music. Women turned him down, politely and rudely. He used to say, plaintively, "No girl will have me." He never married.

 Anton Bruckner to Josefine Lang

 1866

Most honored and amiable Fräulein,

The matter with which I turn to you should not surprise you; no, I am sure that you have long been aware of my constant waiting for you, and so I take up my pen to trouble you. The great and profound request which I take the liberty to address to you herewith, Fräulein Josefine, is this: would Fräulein Josefine kindly give her frank final and decisive answer, in writing, for my future calm, to the question: May I hope and ask your dear parents for your hand? or is it impossible for you to marry me, for lack of affection? Fräulein must see that the question is of utmost importance to me, so I beg you to write as soon as possible the one way or the other, resolutely and decisively. Please may Fräulein Josefine tell this to no one but her parents (please to preserve the strictest secrecy) and take your choice between the two points of the question in agreement with your dear parents. My loyal friend, your honored brother, has already prepared me for everything and has, according to his promise, informed you. Once more I beg you: write frankly and sincerely: either that I may propose, or a complete and permanent refusal (please no compromise to console or evade the point, for it is high time for me), and your feelings will probably not change because Fräulein is reasonable. Fräulein Josefine may say the whole truth without fear because in any case it will give me peace of mind.

Expecting a decisive answer as soon as possible, I kiss your hand.

Anton Bruckner

Friedrich Nietzsche, philosopher of the superman theory, which has been made partly responsible for recent developments in Germany, must have been rather meek in his marriage ambitions. His letter to Miss Trampedach, who had planned to copy Longfellow's poem "Excelsior" for him, lacks the dynamic qualities he described in his ideal **Herrenmensch.** *Mathilde refused to become his superwife. She turned him down politely and married one of his friends, a musical conductor.*

 Friedrich Nietzsche to Mathilde Trampedach

 GENEVA, APRIL 11, 1876

Mein Fräulein,

Tonight you are writing something for me—I should write something for you, too.

Summon all the courage of your heart in order not to be shocked by the question I shall put to you: Will you marry me?

I love you and I feel as if you belong to me already. Not a word about the suddenness of my affection. At least there is no guilt in it, and therefore nothing need be excused. But what I should like to know is whether you feel the same: that we have never been strangers to each other, not for a moment! Do you not also believe that, united, we could become freer and better than separate—excelsior? Will you risk going with me—as with one who struggles valiantly for liberation and progress on all the paths of life and thought? Now be frank with me and keep nothing back; no one knows anything about this letter and my question except our mutual friend Herr von S.

I am leaving tomorrow for Basel. I have to go back. I enclose my Basel address. If you say yes to my question, I shall write to your mother at once. If you can decide quickly either way, a letter can reach me tomorrow until ten at the Hotel Garni de la Poste.

WISHING YOU EVERY HAPPINESS
AND BLISS FOREVER,
Friedrich Nietzsche

Adolf Stoecker, court preacher to William I of Germany, was one of the early pacemakers for Hitler—the first propagator of pan-Germanism and its race theories. For preaching anti-Semitism from the pulpit he was fired by the emperor, but he went into politics and preached it from platform and soapbox. When he asks his lady "in trembling and fear" and, like the early colonists, puts the whole responsibility for his sexual emotions on the Lord, one might well ask whether his political shouting was overcompensated weakness or whether he was just a hypocrite.

 Adolf Stoecker to Anna Krueger

SEGGERDE, MARCH 8, 1864

*H*ighly *Honored Fräulein,*

    I begin this letter with trembling and fear, because your answer to it will bring me the greatest happiness or the most abysmal grief. I fought and wrestled with myself for so long a time, at last after much praying and searching before God, I have found the courage to tell you that I love you with all my heart. I know full well that I ask something great and precious in asking you to love me in return. I also know that I do not deserve to call all this goodness and charm, which my soul has discerned in you, my own. And yet I am compelled by an irresistible force to ask you in the name of the Lord, who has put this great and ardent love into my heart, whether you could reciprocate my affection.

From the first hour that I spent happily in your company, the thought has never left me that your love could make me completely happy—could lift me to Heaven on the wings of an angel and fulfill all my hopes and dreams—that, with you, I could build my house on the foundation of our living Savior, trusting in our unity of faith, love, and prayer.

Accept, then, adored Fräulein, the secret of my life; may the Almighty accept it and weigh it in the hands of His Grace. My soul would exult if He would hear my prayer and incline your heart toward mine; His will be done.

IN SINCERE LOVE AND AFFECTION

YOUR

Adolf

August Strindberg, Swedish dramatist, was born in Stockholm in 1849; his father was a small tradesman, his mother a barmaid. In real life, as on the stage, he rebelled against conventions. Marriage was one of them. He tried it three times, always without success. His first entanglement was Sigrid Wrangel, the wife of an army officer, who divorced her husband to marry him in 1877. He separated from her and married Frieda (Pussy) Uhl, who then took boarders in her little castle on an Austrian lake, while their son worked as a newspaper man. His third failure was a Swedish actress, Harriet Bosse. He grew more and more bitter with every venture in the matrimonial field and took his feelings out in vicious attacks between book covers and in plays.

 August Strindberg to Frieda Uhl

BERLIN, MARCH 11, 1893

*D*ear, good, beautiful, nasty little thing—what are you doing in Munich? Come here to me, we'll put an end to all the gossip, exchange rings, pay our visits, and then we'll be betrothed. If you're afraid of getting married, we can wait a while and test ourselves. After all, a betrothal isn't a rigid bond. You long for me, don't you, and you are afraid it is all only a dream! It is not a dream, only the simple truth, that I love you—I love you, I love you.

It is not "purposeless" to come back to Berlin! You will get a man who loves you and whom you need not despise. A man who will be loyal to you, whether he wants to or not, because you're so young and beautiful and clever and crazy. I even love all the perfectly mad things that you do: when you lie, you lie as only a poet, as only I can lie; I love you because your mouth is so beautiful and your little teeth are so pearly white; when you're angry I love you because your deep eyes spit fire; I love you because you're so horribly clever and greedy, because you write your disagreeable business letters for my sake.

And so: come here and live in the west, so I can live here too, and I'll work, and love you until you are completely crazy.

Now you know everything!

GOOD NIGHT, MY DARLING,

YOUR

August Strindberg

August Strindberg to Friedrich Uhl

 1893

*D*ear *Sir,*

Deeply regretting the indiscretion of the newspapers, which published the engagement of Fräulein Frieda Uhl before I had had an opportunity of writing to you, I beg to ask your approval of this marriage.

An indisposition frustrated my hopes of calling on you in Vienna; it chained me to my bed during these last days.

As my affairs tie me to Berlin, I would like to ask you to permit your daughter to take up her residence here, as soon as possible, again, so that we can together prepare everything for the wedding, which we wish to celebrate in May.

Looking forward to your kind answer, I beg you to believe in my gratitude and affection.

August Strindberg

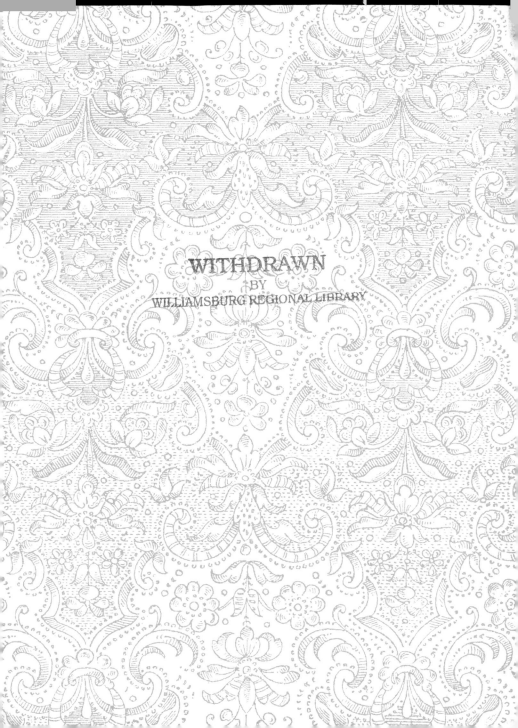
WITHDRAWN
BY
WILLIAMSBURG REGIONAL LIBRARY